Seeing Both Sides

Smartphones in Class, Yes or No

Reese Everett

Rourke
Educational Media

rourkeeducationalmedia.com

*Scan for Related Titles
and Teacher Resources*

Before Reading:

Building Academic Vocabulary and Background Knowledge

Before reading a book, it is important to tap into what your child or students already know about the topic. This will help them develop their vocabulary, increase their reading comprehension, and make connections across the curriculum.

1. *Look at the cover of the book. What will this book be about?*
2. *What do you already know about the topic?*
3. *Let's study the Table of Contents. What will you learn about in the book's chapters?*
4. *What would you like to learn about this topic? Do you think you might learn about it from this book? Why or why not?*
5. *Use a reading journal to write about your knowledge of this topic. Record what you already know about the topic and what you hope to learn about the topic.*
6. *Read the book.*
7. *In your reading journal, record what you learned about the topic and your response to the book.*
8. *After reading the book complete the activities below.*

Content Area Vocabulary
Read the list. What do these words mean?

advantages
cyberbullying
debate
essential
hamper
invaluable
neuroscientists
peers
stance

After Reading:

Comprehension and Extension Activity

After reading the book, work on the following questions with your child or students in order to check their level of reading comprehension and content mastery.

1. *What is an opinion? (Summarize)*
2. *Explain why two people might have the same opinion for different reasons. (Infer)*
3. *How can smartphones help students concentrate in class? (Asking questions)*
4. *Have you ever used a smartphone to do your schoolwork? What did you use it for? (Text to self connection)*
5. *What are some ways smartphones can distract students in class? (Asking questions)*

Extension Activity

Before starting your homework, put a blank sheet of paper next to you. Mark the paper each time you pick up your smartphone to do something that doesn't relate to your homework. Tally the marks when you are finished. How many times did you pick up your phone? Do you think you might complete your homework faster and do a better job if you put the phone away? Why or why not?

Table of Contents

Taking Sides.. 4

Smartphones in Class? Yes, Please! 6

Smartphones in Class? No Way! 17

Your Turn.. 28

Glossary 30

Index... 31

Show What You Know.. 31

Websites to Visit.. 31

About the Author 32

Taking Sides

Many students have smartphones, but the devices are not always welcome in classrooms. Should they be?

People have different opinions about students using smartphones at school. An opinion is someone's belief based on their knowledge and experiences. Sometimes people change their minds when they get more information. Sometimes they change their minds when they consider something from a different point of view.

What do you think about students using smartphones in class? Are the devices helpful or a distraction? Why do you think so?

Let's look at some arguments from different sides of the **debate**. Then you can share your own opinion.

Reality ✓

Researchers say about half of elementary school students in the U.S. use smartphones, and the number grows every year.

Smartphones in Class? Yes, Please!

Students should always be encouraged to use their smartphones in the classroom. The devices are valuable educational tools that provide **advantages** for students and cost nothing for the school.

Computers are **essential** in every classroom, but it is rare to have a computer for every student. Allowing them to use their smartphones for online research frees up the computers for those who don't have the devices.

In addition to Internet access, smartphone apps let students type and edit documents, create spreadsheets, and produce videos. Instead of 30 students sharing a couple of classroom computers, students can use their smartphones to complete and share projects.

Reality ✓

A majority of teachers think students are more productive because of technology used in the classroom.

Smartphones also make students' work portable. There is no need to save anything on a flash drive to take home; instead, everything you need to complete your work is right on your phone. When you're ready to present it, you can plug your smartphone into the classroom projector.

Students spend about 35 hours at school each week. Learning is a full-time job! Smartphones can help them stay organized for success. Students can snap a picture of homework assignment instructions. They can also keep track of due dates on a smartphone calendar.

Teachers can use smartphone apps to turn a classroom into a high-tech, interactive environment that gets kids excited to participate. Students can click answers on their phones as questions are asked aloud.

Students can use their smartphones to communicate through text or email with their teachers about assignments. They can also use them to let the teacher know something they may not feel comfortable speaking up about.

Reality ✓
Sometimes students don't want to ask or answer questions because they fear embarrassment. Texting and interactive apps lets them participate without the worry.

Students study several subjects every day. Each subject requires a textbook. Textbooks are heavy, can be easily damaged, and are expensive to provide for every student.

Students can use their smartphones to access electronic versions of the same books, which can't be ripped or lost. This can save the school money. It's also much easier to carry one smartphone than seven textbooks, which saves students' backs!

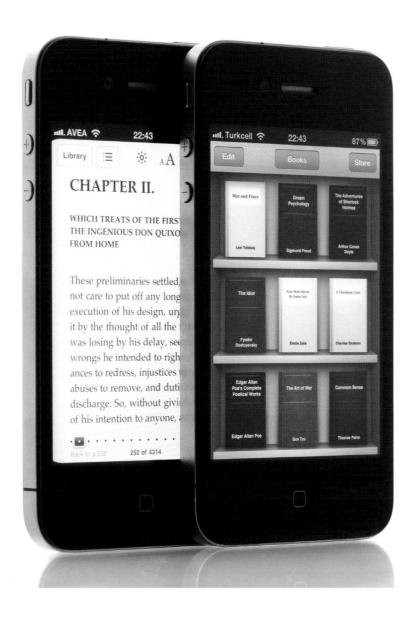

A classmate's cough, the shuffle of footsteps, a door opening and closing–these little things are enough to distract even the most focused students. A smartphone can be a useful tool to drown out the distraction. Some teachers allow students to plug in headphones and listen to music while they work. This lets them tune out annoyances and tune into learning.

Some people argue that students will use their smartphones to text or play games in class instead of paying attention. But students who are not engaged in a lesson will always find ways to amuse themselves. An electronic device doesn't distract students any more than a pencil and paper or their own thoughts might.

The overall benefits outweigh any negative effects these devices may have on a few students. For students who are interested in learning, they are an **invaluable** tool.

Smartphones are a library, planner, camera, radio, and communication tool bundled into one device that fits in your pocket. Free apps turn them into word processors and video editing tools, too! If students have their own smartphones, why would schools not want them to use something that puts everything they need at their fingertips?

Reality ✓

Many schools in the U.S. have adopted BYOD, or Bring Your Own Device, policies. Some schools provide devices, such as tablets, for students who don't have their own.

Smartphones in Class? No Way!

Many students have their own smartphones, but allowing them in the classroom is not a good idea. Experts say children spend about six hours a day staring  at screens, whether it's the TV, a smartphone, or a tablet. School should be a place where students learn through listening, speaking, and hands-on activities that don't require an electronic device.

Schools should encourage face-to face interaction between students and teachers, not electronic communication. Students need to learn how to speak and listen to **peers** and adults. Even the smartest people in the world must be good communicators, otherwise no one can benefit from their knowledge.

School is where young people learn to interact effectively with others. Allowing them to hide behind their smartphones to communicate with classmates and teachers will **hamper** their social skills.

Reality ✓

Voice tone and body language are important parts of communication that can't be conveyed in texts and emails. Sometimes this can lead to a misunderstanding.

Many people use their smartphones for texting and social media sites. This is not a productive use of time. Allowing smartphones in class will just mean more of students' valuable time will be wasted when they should be learning.

Reality ✓

Some health experts say smartphone use can cause bad posture, because you are looking down—putting a strain on your neck—while using it.

Students who are struggling in school already may fall more behind if they are allowed to use their smartphone. Rather than using it for assignments, they may be tempted to surf the Internet or play games. Schools should only allow tools in the classroom that benefit every student, and should never encourage anything that has the potential to disrupt their studies.

Bullying can be a problem at schools. Smartphones make it easy for someone to bully another student without opening their mouth or causing a scene. Schools can't monitor what is done online when students are at home, but they should prevent bullying at school. Banning smartphones prevents **cyberbullying** that might occur during the school day.

Reality ✓

In a recent study, more than half of the young people surveyed said they'd been cyberbullied.

What happens when a student's phone breaks? Imagine a student drops their phone on the floor, and another student steps on it accidentally. Or perhaps the phone gets something spilled on it. Who is responsible for fixing it? If the devices are used for schoolwork, the school may be liable for the cost of fixing or replacing the smartphone. This could cost schools a lot of money.

People with smartphones tend to check them constantly rather than paying attention to what's going on around them. They miss out on noticing things that can make them smarter, more creative, and more thoughtful.

And finally, the simplest reason smartphones should not
be allowed in the classroom: every student doesn't have one.
It's not fair to allow devices that could give some students
advantages over others.

If students are allowed to use their smartphones at school to do their work, what happens to those who don't own one? They will be limited to the class computer, which they will have to share with other students. They won't have access to a camera and photo editing apps. And they won't be able to easily take their work home with them to complete. They will have less time and resources to use, which could affect the outcome of their projects and their grades.

Students should have equal access to the resources needed to complete their schoolwork. Allowing students to use their smartphones in class isn't fair to those who don't have them.

Reality ✓

Some **neuroscientists** say too much smartphone use can hamper balanced brain development.

Your Turn

What is your **stance** on using smartphones in class now that you've read arguments for and against it? Each side used reasons, facts, and examples. Which side do you think had the strongest points? What would you add?

Write about your opinion, and include reasons and supporting information. You may also want to include stories from your experiences as a student, supporting your position with real-world, personal examples.

Telling Your Side: Writing Opinion Pieces

- Tell your opinion first. Use phrases such as:
- *I like* _____.
- *I think* ____.
- _____ *is the best* _____.
- Give multiple reasons to support your opinion. Use facts and relevant information instead of stating your feelings.
- Use the words *and*, *because*, and *also* to connect your opinion to your reasons.
- Clarify or explain your facts by using the phrases *for example* or *such as*.
- Compare your opinion to a different opinion. Then point out reasons that your opinion is better. You can use phrases such as:
- *Some people think_____, but I disagree because* _____.
- _____ *is better than* _____ *because* _____.
- Give examples of positive outcomes if the reader agrees with your opinion. For example, you can use the phrase, *If* _____ *then* _____.
- Use a personal story about your own experiences with your topic. For example, if you are writing about your opinion on after-school sports, you can write about your own experiences with after-school sports activities.
- Finish your opinion piece with a strong conclusion that highlights your strongest arguments. Restate your opinion so your reader remembers how you feel.

Glossary

advantages (ad-vuhn-TAY-juhs): things that help you or put you ahead

cyberbullying (SYE-bur-bul-EE-ing): using electronic communication to harass someone

debate (duh-bayt): a discussion on a topic with both sides represented

essential (i-SEN-shuhl): necessary or very important

hamper (HAM-pur): to make it difficult for something to succeed

invaluable (in-VAL-yu-buhl): indispensable, valuable, or necessary

neuroscientists (noor-oh-SYE-uhn-tists): scientists that study the brain

peers (peers): people of the same age or ranking, such as school grade level

stance (stants): emotional or intellectual attitude; a publicly stated opinion

Index

access 7, 13, 26, 27

apps 7, 10 11, 16, 26

communicate 11, 19

cyberbullying 22

Internet 7, 21

organized 9

research 6

researchers 5

resources 26, 27

social media 20

texting 11, 20

Show What You Know

1. How does using information from experts help support your opinion?

2. Why should you use personal examples to explain your position on a topic?

3. Why is it important to use facts and information in opinion pieces rather than just talking about the way a topic makes you feel?

4. Do you think it is easy to persuade people to change their opinion? Why or why not?

5. Is it possible to agree with points on both sides of an issue?

Websites to Visit

www.stopbullying.gov/cyberbullying

www.quandarygame.org

www.readwritethink.org/classroom-resources/student-interactives/fact-fragment-frenzy-30013.html

About the Author

Reese Everett is a writer, editor, and journalist in sunny Tampa, Florida. She enjoys funny movies, long days at the beach, and hanging out with her four kids. She has a smartphone that she uses for everything. Sometimes her kids have to remind her to put it down.

Meet The Author!
www.meetREMauthors.com

www.rourkeeducationalmedia.com

PHOTO CREDITS: Cover (top): ©DusanManic; cover (bottom): ©LisaHoward; page 1: ©fotostorm; page 3: ©Pamela Moore; page 4: ©jjshawl4; page 5: ©rulsoft; page 5 (bottom), 7, 11, 16, 19, 20, 22, 27: ©loops7; page 6: ©numbeos; page 7, 11, 19: ©Steve Debenport; page 8: ©fifoprod; page 9: ©mediaphotos; page 9 (bottom): ©bgblue; page 10, 21: ©leonrado Patrizi; page 12: ©muratseyit; page 13: ©Vunus Arakon; page 14: ©mediaphotos; page 15: ©Svetiana Braun; page 16: ©Merve Karahn; page 17: ©Susan Chiang; page 17 (bottom): ©Richard Goerg; page 18: ©Cathy Yeulet; page 20, 26: ©Catherine Lane; page 22, 24: ©MachineHeadz; page 23: ©mugensx; page 25: ©lev dolgachev; page 27: ©lisafx; page 28: ©monkeybusinessimages

Edited by: Keli Sipperley

Cover design and Interior design by: Rhea Magaro

Library of Congress PCN Data

Smartphones in Class, Yes or No / Reese Everett
(Seeing Both Sides)
ISBN 978-1-68191-382-7 (hard cover)
ISBN 978-1-68191-424-4(soft cover)
ISBN 978-1-68191-464-0(e-Book)
Library of Congress Control Number: 2015951549

Also Available as:

Printed in the United States of America, North Mankato, Minnesota